The Museum of Primitive Art • *Lecture Series Number Three*
TECHNIQUE & PERSONALITY IN PRIMITIVE ART

TECHNIQUE &

Distributed by the New York Graphic Society, 1963

PERSONALITY

Margaret Mead • Junius B. Bird • Hans Himmelheber
THE MUSEUM OF PRIMITIVE ART, NEW YORK

$$\frac{N}{5\,3/0}$$

$$M\,36$$

48309

Distributed by the New York Graphic Society
Copyright 1963, The Museum of Primitive Art
Printed in the United States of America by Davis, Delaney, Inc.
Library of Congress Card Number: 63-19321

CONTENTS

Margaret Mead
THE BARK PAINTINGS OF
THE MOUNTAIN ARAPESH
OF NEW GUINEA

The Sepik-Aitape district of North East New Guinea is famous for the distinctive and contrasting artistic forms that are found among its many linguistic groups, each of which conducts extensive trade with the whole area. Analysis shows that these cultures may be divided into cultures with highly distinctive styles — like the lake-dwelling Tchambuli and Aibom peoples with styles so distinctive that placement of a mask or a carved wooden hook is never in doubt; cultures which combine a distinctive local style with extensive and eclectic imports from other peoples — like the Iatmul of the Middle Sepik River; and cultures with very little of their own that is either distinctive or elaborated — like the Mountain Arapesh and other mountain peoples. The first two groups are easy to characterize by the objects that they make, and even without any field material on the activities of the artists it is possible from the collections that reach a museum to make an adequate statement about style. But for people like the Arapesh who have no distinctive style of decoration in any form that can be collected and subsequently studied, we are up against a very different problem. Simple statements that they are an importing people and rely on their neighbors for decorated objects, and themselves occasionally decorate a single bark slab in some ill-defined way, or scribble traditional stick figures on the bark shingles of the houses, are practically all that can be made. Yet, in the study of art, the people who produce so slightly, in an area where there are many models, are as interesting to science as those who decorate their houses and their club houses with beautifully executed carvings and paintings. The absence of a developed art, in an area where the achievements of each people in any field are regarded as the potential cultural acquisitions of all the other people, should, if investigated, throw light on the necessary conditions for producing artistic work, or upon those cultural conditions that discourage production. But such investigations require a longer and more intensified field work than that which is sufficient to bring back a well-documented set of designs.

8

The Mountain Arapesh[1] live in small scattered settlements. They are gardeners and sago workers, able to make simple tools and weapons, but depending upon trade for objects that are well decorated or finely made. Directly beyond them in the mountains live the Plains Arapesh, studied by Dr. Phyllis Kaberry[2] and the Abelam studied by Mr. Anthony Forge,[3] who build large men's houses, very tall with sharply sloping ridgepoles, the fronts of which are transversely panelled with rows of very impressive, brightly colored, painted designs on sago bark, fastened to a scaffolding. The mountain people who travel inland on expeditions to make propitiatory payments to the Plains sorcerers have seen these great spectacular men's houses, rising sixty and seventy feet out of the clump of village trees. They know how the paintings are made, what clays are used, and they have reduced the process which in the interior involves the production of a whole facade to the simplest unit — a flattened sago bark spathe, some eighteen inches wide and three to four feet long. The painting is simply called by the word for such a flattened spathe *(bāg* or *baiyas)*. Occasionally mountain men attempted such painting. If successful, the painting can be used to decorate the very modest men's houses which they sometimes build in connection with a boys' initiation ceremony. Where the rows of painted faces and designs were an integral part of the towering men's houses of the Plains Arapesh and the Abelam, they were a casual, inessential embellishment of the men's houses of the mountains. Similarly with a locality of some two hundred people, there might or there might not be, someone who "knew how" to make a *bāg* — roughly a synonym for "known to have done so." The Arapesh spend a great deal of time walking from place to place, to help out a relative, plant another small garden, spend a few days hunting in the deep bush. Almost every elaborate cultural activity, a ritual, painting some embellishment for the rarely built men's houses, is performed so infrequently that any young man may grow up without having seen some essential part of it. There is a great casualness about details, a great willingness

9

to substitute one element for another, a lack of emphasis on precision or form. The people import new charms, new rituals, new dances, and in a few years the dances have disappeared or disintegrated into small bits; new seeds are imported and lost. They combine a high degree of hospitality to the new with a lack of belief in their own capacities to reproduce the cultural activities of other groups, and a lack of institutionalized ways of holding on to new cultural acquisitions. Typically, the last man who has done something — who "knows how" — will become the master of the next ceremony; only a man who has purified himself from the ghost of the man whose widow he wishes to marry, either learns, or can pass on, the appropriate ritual. Quite understandably, young men of imagination live in a kind of low level terror that some essential detail will get away from them altogether.

Design elements, which are sometimes used in the bark paintings, are carried along fairly consistently in the children's scribbling with bits of charcoal on the sides of houses — made of the same sago bark that is used to make a bark slab painting — and girls and women pass the time by making these drawings while confined in menstrual huts, and without occupation. These *plate 1* stick drawings are fully stylized and anyone can tell whether a given drawing is a star, a dog, a man or lizard. They contrast with the lesser stylization and vague and contradictory and shifting interpretations that are given when bark paintings are made in part imitation of the bark paintings of the inland people. This carrying along of a relatively firm, very simple core of artistic behavior, within a culture in which there are frequent shifts in style, may have important consequences, both in providing a kind of integrating ethos, and preventing the development of clearer and more developed styles. It may also be comparable to the preservation of singing styles in lullabies,[4] or the preservation of a core vocabulary in diverging dialects,[5] both of which depend upon relationships between women and small children. Among the Mountain Arapesh the men have not

10

Plate 1. Children's drawings, Alitoa

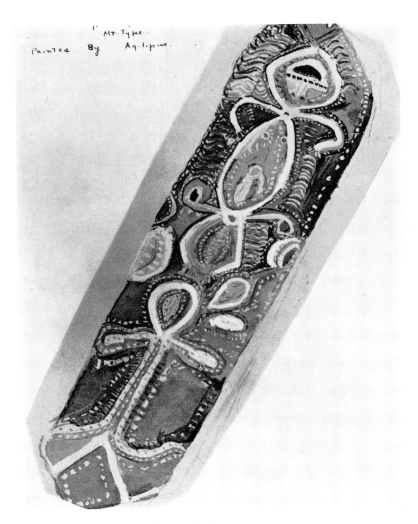

Plate 2. Painting by Agilipwe of Alitoa

developed any contrasting ethos to that of the women, and both sexes are characterized by mild, responsive, cherishing behavior.

Within such a setting, the only way to study artistic behavior is actually to see an artist working — as happens very rarely.

In the locality of Alitoa in 1931-32, there were two men who admittedly knew how to paint a bark slab: Agilipwe, a bad-tempered old man suffering from a chronic framboesia sore; and Baimal, a gentle, lively, intelligent man, with much of the intensity and sensitivity which is traditionally associated with the temperament of the artist. While we were in Alitoa in 1932, the extensive collection of Plains Arapesh paintings which had been made for the American Museum of Natural History by Dr. R. F. Fortune was brought into the mountain village and spread out there for reconditioning. This display—which would never have occurred under aboriginal conditions — stimulated the interest of the people so that they attempted several paintings.

I was able to collect several slabs, and also to get some *plate 2* paintings done on paper. The following account of procedures combines interviewing and observation, but the additional information could not have been collected by interviewing alone, or on the basis of finished specimens. It was only possible to get even this meager account by tracing the actual steps, the shifts and changes of plan between the painter and his helper, and by subsequent discussions on the basis of the work that had been carefully recorded.

The field used for the painting is the flattened interior bark of the curved sago palm spathe, after the outer bark and most of the pith has been cut away. This is then smoked, pith side down, over a fire of coconut palm leaves so that it is possible to straighten the bark. If the plan is to decorate the outer corner of a house, it is not straightened. The typical shape is shieldlike, straight across the top, with a blunt point at the bottom. After it has been smoked and all pith removed, it is placed smooth side down in the sun, with stones put on it to weigh it down. The largest stones are put in the place which needs most straightening. A branch of the *dimi*[6] tree is beaten with a stone, and wrung out, either in a piece of coconut palm sheath, or simply with the hands. After most of the sap has been squeezed out, the remainder of the sap is squeezed into a coconut shell or directly on to the bark slab, and rubbed over its surface either with the bare hands, or alternatively the shredded beaten bundle of *dimi* branches is scrubbed directly onto the bark. If *dimi* is not available, the sap of the breadfruit tree can be used. Either kind of sap serves to make a surface to which the clay paint will adhere. The entire surface is then coated with a powder made from scraped soft stone, *adag,* obtained from the Sulum River. For brushes the tail feather of the pigeon, *manyin,* or the *nauwitep* bird can be used. These are preferred but any quill feathers will do. Sometimes a piece of sago stem is pounded and used for coarse work. Sometimes the *adag* coating is simply scrubbed on with the hand and sometimes it is omitted altogether. If the *adag* wash, which dries as pale steel gray, is used, the spaces on which no further painting is done give the slab painting a light effect. If the *adag* wash is omitted, the dark, mahogany-like color of the sago bark gives the whole slab a somber effect. When the painting is finished, it is set in the sun to dry, except in the cases where an undecorated bark slab has been fastened to the corner of the house, for future decoration.

The other materials with which a painter must provide himself are a flat stone, to use as a palette for mixing colors, a shell *(yalug)* or knife for scraping paints, charcoal made of burned *alop* wood, scrubbed down with water on the stone palette or black clay, three kinds of red clay, *bulum, ausibah* and *ogi'a* obtained from the seaward people, yellow clay, *awoku,* obtained from the next village, Liwo, and two white clays, *lahein,* scraped and mixed with water, giving a creamy tone, and *silag* dipped in water and scrubbed on the stone palette.

When the painter is ready to work he divides the field roughly, either by delineating a number of areas or by placing a thematic sketch (for a cassowary or phalanger, and so on) in the middle.

The field may be divided up lightly, and the theme worked

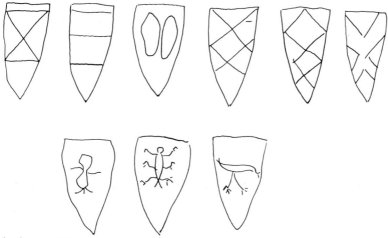

in later. Then the painter sets to work. He may work alone, or with one or more helpers. Bystanders may give advice but the man who is painting *(wutam)* the slab is deferred to. The number of people who will work at once is dictated by the number of brushes to hand. The painter sets to work on details, doing a patch here and a patch there, and directing his helpers. He works from detail to detail so that a large section of the decorative field is unplanned. Later miniature drawings may be fitted into empty spaces, or half-hearted attempts at new themes may be made, abandoned, and simply painted over, but if the painter decides that he has made a mistake in the use of color, the paint is carefully scraped off. This is in keeping with the greater emphasis on color rather than form. In matters of form the Arapesh painters are imitative and unimaginative. When I supplied them with rectangular pieces of drawing paper, they responded to the new shape by distorting the familiar design elements. Only when I cut paper into the shield shape of their own bark slabs were they able to reproduce their own designs with traditional proportions.[7] Where color was concerned they showed far greater sensitivity. When some of the younger men began using the entire range of colors in my box of paints, splashing purple and green on, in happy disregard of the traditional low toned palette, Baimal muttered disapprovingly, *"she lupa"* a phrase used for the fighting of dogs.

If a white outlining of field divisions or theme is made, the water separates from the white clay and runs down each side of the line and makes a dark border. Sometimes this is not filled in completely and forms a kind of tenuous accent. This water border also suggests accents in the designs themselves. If black is used in outlining — a much less frequent choice — this effect is not produced.

One color can be superimposed upon another, as in oil painting, without loss if a dark color is put over a light one, but when a light color is put over a dark one, a heavy coat is necessary. This is likely to produce a smeary effect, as in the space between the jaws of the cassowary. Willingness to put one color over another means that no allowance needs to be made for later changes of plan, and mistakes are not serious. An apprentice endeavoring to keep up with an experienced painter will correct his mistakes but an experienced painter may actually capitalize on them, letting his imagination follow on the erroneous lead.

If the paint is too thick it can be smoothed by a light scraping off of lumps. Several kinds of each color are used, charcoal as well as black clay, and the painter's choice of colors is as often dictated by his supply of particular paints as by aesthetic considerations. Also a painting may be begun with one shade of red and finished with another.

There are a variety of small conventional elements that can be used in these paintings, many of which have one or more conventional significances loosely attached to them.

When purely conventional elements are used, the design elements may be interpreted by the artists in a variety of ways; the series of different sized diamond shapes may be interpreted as a human being, and smaller elements may be said to be human breasts, testicles, and so on. The painter himself will change his

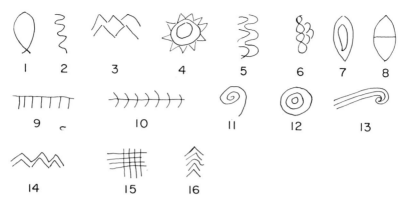

1. a taro; 2. vine or snake; 3. —; 4. sun, moon or morning star; 5. snake; 6. taro (*bagihas*) or shell rings; 7. —; 8. yam; 9. face painting design or a palm leaf; 10. palm leaf; 11. vine tendril; 12. sun, moon, or morning star; 13. vine; 14. —; 15. ribs; 16. —.

mind over night and give new interpretations, and other people will not venture them at all. Formal field dividing lines may be interpreted as snakes. If no stereotyped symbolic element is present the interpretation of a single figure may vary through all the available animals. Except where a theme element is unusually clear, everyone except the painter himself will reply to questions about the subject matter with: "I don't understand the [intent of the] man who made it." So Baimal made a pair of paintings, and twice reversed his decision as to which was male and which was female.

In 1931 we did not have the recording devices that we have today, no method of taking rapid sequences of stills, no cine camera that could be used effectively in field work, no color film. I had to record all the stages by hand, and — using water colors — paint in miniature each stage of the proceedings. I reproduce here the sequence of the painting of a bark slab, by these two men from a poor, importing culture, one of whom I have called the "master" because in his behavior there were echoes of the behavior of master painters found in other parts of the area; the other I have called the "apprentice" as he had not painted before but was eager to learn. When the procedure was finished, my miniature naturally looked finer than the large crude painting in clay: Baimal looked at it, muttered "Women, women," and his manhood sorely injured, deserted the village for several days. The conversation was recorded verbatim at the time, in the Arapesh language, and is translated here.

[1] Margaret Mead. The Mountain Arapesh. American Museum of Natural History, Anthropological Papers 36, 1938: 139-349; 37, 1940: 317-451; 40, 1947: 159-420; 41, 1949: 285-390.

[2] Phyllis M. Kaberry. The Abelam tribe, Sepik District, New Guinea: A Preliminary Report. Oceania 11, 1941: 233-258, 345-367.
—. Law and political organization in the Abelam tribe, New Guinea. Oceania 12, 1941-2: 79-95, 209-225, 331-363.

[3] Anthony Forge. Notes on eastern Abelam designs painted on paper. In Three regions of Melanesian art, by Anthony Forge and Raymond Clausen. New York, 1960: 12-15.

[4] Alan Lomax. Folk Song Style. American Anthropologist 61, 1959: 927-954.
—. Song Structure and Social Structure. Ethnology 1, 1962: 425-451.

[5] R. B. Lees. The basis of glottochronology. Language 29, 1953: 113-137.

[6] Our botanical collection was damaged by water so that I have only the native names for plants and trees.

[7] Anthony Forge's collection of miniature paintings of Abelam housefront units (loc. cit.) does not suffer from the contrasts in shapes because the typical housefront unit was rectangular and made of two or more pieces of sago bark, stitched together.

Plate 3. Bark painting, cassowary theme. 44½" high by 14" wide. American Museum of Natural History, New York 80.0-7293

19

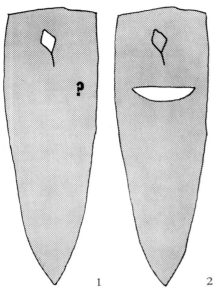

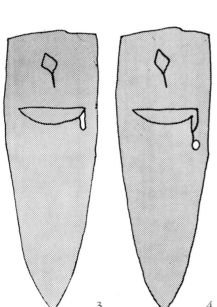

1 2

3 4

Cassowary theme (plate 3)

While A *smokes leaves,* M *sits and traces designs in the air over* bāg *with a feather. After coating of* adag *has dried . . .*

M "I'll make a snake."

O "But you said you'd make a cassowary."

M "All right, I'll make a cassowary." *Makes* (1) *and says,* "This paint is bad."
A *takes his brush and helps; thickens line.*

A "Shouldn't its head be over here?" *Draws line in* (2).

M "I can go this way with head here" (3). *Then* A *does* (4). "Mm! Pretty small." *Both enlarge neck.*

ABBREVIATIONS USED:

HO — *Helpful Onlooker*
O — *Onlooker*
A — *Apprentice*
M — *Master*
P — *Passerby*

M "This is the neck."
M *does* (5).

A "That's too big."
(Note change in roles, because M *uncertain about cassowary.)* M *runs hand along upper back.*

M "Legs can go here? This is the head."
But A *puts in one leg, running down, and* M *adds left leg* (6). M *lengthens his left leg and* A *lengthens his, ignoring former attempt at claw* (7). A *cleans off error* (6). M *draws claw.* A *draws long, long claws* (8). M *underlines neck in red* (8). A *does jaws in black.* M *approves.*

M "Yes, in black. Yes, like that."

A "Enough."
M *puts red in jaw.*

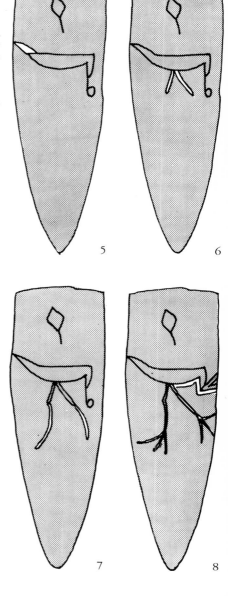

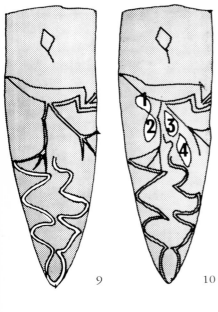

9   10

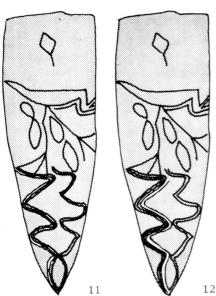

11   12

M "The mouth, I understand."
A *increases width of line of red.*

M "Be careful, there's not much paint."
M *adds lines to back.*

A "Put some dots in jaws?"
M *stands off and looks at it.*

A "Make the mouth bigger front."
M *mixes some white paint and sketches in* (9).

M "It's her eggs."
M *does 1, 2, 3, 4* (10).

M "This is a vine."

A "Shall I do this in red?"

M "Yes."
M *is finishing 3 in* (10). A *does* (11).

P "A snake?"

M "Yes."
M *does* (12) *in yellow.*

A "We'll put red inside over there and outside here?"

22

M "Yes."
   A *puts in red* (13).

M "Look out there," *as A gets red on white.* "Yes, like that, like that."

A "Shall I do 1 and 2 (13)?"

M "No, I'll do it later in red."
   M *puts yellow on right side* (13).

A "Shall I do edge of cassowary's legs in red?"

M "All right."
   A *does* (14). M *does* (15). A *has finished outlining one leg on both sides; goes to neck, which M continues, putting in yellow of* (15).

A "White here?" *(between jaws of cassowary).*

M "Yes."

M "Later I'll put red here (16). No, you do it."
   A *does.* M *puts in yellow oval while A does two red.* M *puts in red curlicues, then yellow on each side* (16).

13

14

15

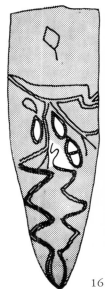

16

17

18

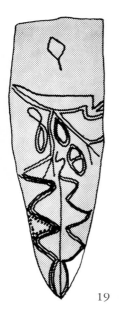

19

20

M "I'll put black paint and white dots in here."
A starts with white.

M "That white is bad; go and get some *silag* out of the palm spathe."
A gets silag *and scrapes it down with water.*

M "That's no good either. It has dirt in it." *He cuts it in half with his knife, then comes and scrapes* A's *dirty mixture off stone. Dips stone in water and scrubs it hard. A takes feather and starts in to paint as shown in* (17).

M "No, here," *(in right row).*
M's *yellow is finished; scrapes.*
"I'll put yellow here," *uses crack in* bāg *as dividing line* (18). M *puts in 2 and 3* (18).

A "What shall I put here?"

M "Where?"

A "Here."

M "Black."
A scrapes some black.

M "Be careful. Let the red *(outline)* stay. Make it small."
M *does yellow of* (19). *Then goes on mixing black.*

A "What shall I put here?"

M "Red?"

A *"You* know. There are many paints."

M *does black* (20). A *does red of* (20). M *traces a red line up to cassowary's leg.*

A "Shall I fill this in?" *(next triangle above red,* 20).

M "No, not yet."

A "I'll do this." (21).
Then M *puts in lines in* (22). *Then* M *does lines as in* (23). M *tells* A *to put in black* (24) *lower and then upper, then* M *tells* A *to put yellow lower then upper. Then* M *does white* (25).

21

22

23

24

25

26

27

28

A "Now what shall I do?"

M "Put yellow here" (25, *left side*). *Then* M *reaches over and reinforces white line and says to* A,

M "Fill that in with yellow." M *then puts in white triangles* (25, *1 and 2*). *Then he feels about and finally decides on place to join triangle to double ovals and does lines of* (26). A *puts yellow line in one oval* (26).

M "You fill these *(left side triangles)* in with dots."

A "I'll go over and sit over there, and you come over here." A *moves over and scrubs out some more white paint.* A *starts in this triangle* (27, 2) *to put in white dots.* M *puts in yellow* (27), *then puts in red. Then* M *improves outline of lower jaw.* A *does dots in* (27, 1) M *puts red outlines around black leg.*

A "Shall I do another line of this?"

M "Do along edge." M *does 1* (28), *then 2, then 3 in red.* A *puts in white dots as shown.*

Then M *does* (29) *upper yellow, then lower.* A *puts dots along red line to claw on right side, then as* M *indicates dots outer edge left cassowary leg.* M *puts yellow under cassowary's leg* (30). A *puts in red dots. Then* M *puts in triangles. Then* A *puts white dots in the two black triangles. Then* M *does* (31). *Tells* A *to do remaining space in white.*

Pause here while they eat.

Now M *attacks upper space in which false beginning still remains.* A *strengthens line in* (31) *after* M *does all the space dividing done in white* (32, 33).

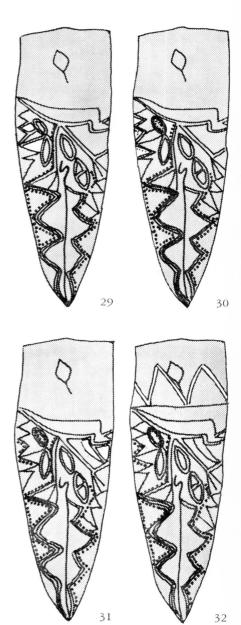

29   30

31   32

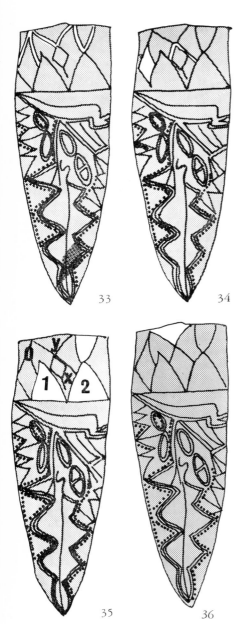

33   34

35   36

A   "Shall I do this (34) in yellow?"

M   "Yes."

M *puts in two lines* (34). A *does* (35, 1) *in red.*

M   "Fill in these triangles in red, yellow, and black, and I'll come back and finish it." *Yields his brush to* A-2, *a still younger boy.* A *does* (35, 2) *in red.* A-2 *does black* (35), *runs over a line.* A *scolds him.* A-2 *starts to put black in triangle marked* x.

A "No, here," *(in triangle marked y).*

A *suggests leaving margin above black triangle in* (36). *He tends to stops now and supervise* A-2. *They fill in all triangles except* 1 *and* 2 (37), *and paint white over cassowary, and then* M *comes and puts dots along cassowary's body, then puts in dots between cassowary's claws, then in small black triangles, then calls* A *back to do* 1 *and* 2 (38).

37   38

Conventional design (plate 4)

M *began at 8:00 A.M. in the morn-ing.* Smoked, dimi'd, *and washed in* adag *by himself. After* (2) *two Liwo onlookers joined him. He did* (3), *1 and 2, and said he'd not put other circle designs in, but on-looker suggested putting in 3, 4, 5, and 6. Next he drew dividing lines through the centers of 1 and 2* (4).

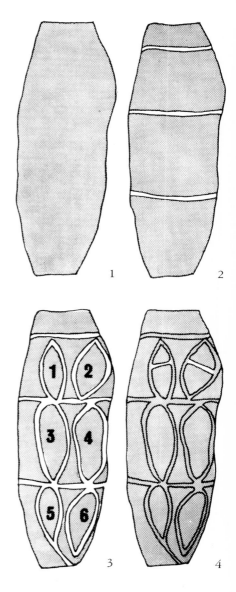

Plate 4. Bark painting, conventional design. 43¾" high by 15" wide. American Museum of Natural History, New York 80.0-7294

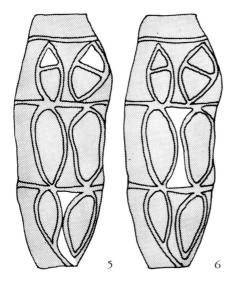

5   6

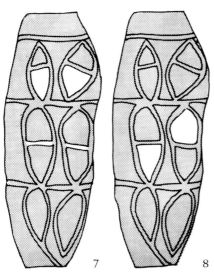

7   8

HO "Shall I put red here (5)?"

M   "Yes, in both."
Meanwhile he puts in yellow (5) and black (6).

HO "What shall I do with these? *(lower halves, upper circles)* Black?"

M   "I don't know, let's see. Wait. Later."

HO "And what are you going to do with these? *(middle circles)* Put white in here?"
Returns to top circle while M *continues to paint (6) and is absorbed by it.*

HO "How about this?" *Puts a little yellow in lower section's top circle.*

M   "Yes, that's all right. Do them both like that."
HO does (7) and M completes (6).

HO "Shall I do this in red?" *(of two central circles, lower section).*

M   "Yes, like the others."

HO "Entirely like the others?"

M "Yes."

HO *begins to do yellow of* (8). M *does red of* (8). A *does red* (9). M *does yellow.* M *now turns the* bāg *around so top is near him and divides two lowest ovals in white; others were done in black* (10). A *is preparing to use quill end on black paint* (11).

A "Shall I make this black?"

M "Yes. No, here."

A *does it in black* (12). M *does little triangles* (a) *and* (b) *in yellow.*

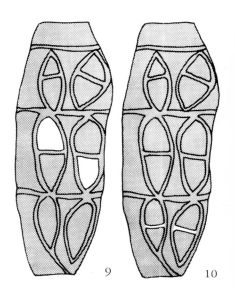

9   10

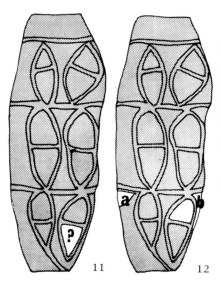

11   12

33

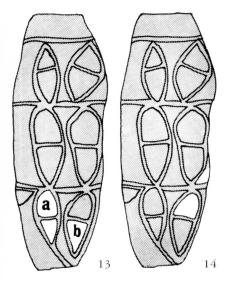

13   14

M "Do the other one black, down below."

M *does this in red and starts (b) in red* (13). *A finishes (b) lower section left lower oval in red. A leaves.* M *puts in black* (14). *Then* M *goes over* A's *work in black, smoothing it. Then turns the* bāg *around and looks at it.*

This is how it looks (15).

M *puts in* (17) *then* (16) *in white (the triangular lines).* A *returns.* M *tells* A *to do red* (17). *He does yellow.*

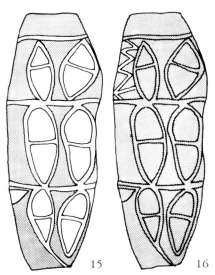

15   16

A "Yellow here?"

M "Yes."

A "How are you going to make this come out?"

M "Not yet. Later."

A "Do it so I'll see."

M "Yes, like that. Yes, yellow!"

A "Here." (20, a)

M "Yes. And black there." (20, c)

A "And what here?"

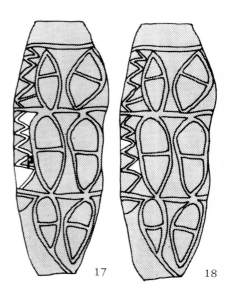

17   18

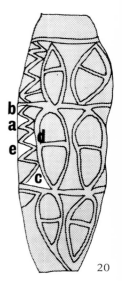

20

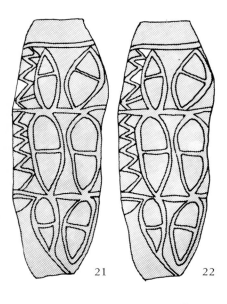

21   22

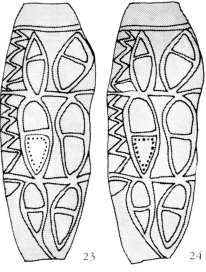

23   24

M "Later on, not yet. Make the black better."
M does black while A does yellow. M does (a) and (b) in black.

A "Red here?"

M "Yes."
M sits and looks at it. Puts in yellow (21).

M *Meditatively,* "Later I'll put dots in here." *(of two lowest ovals) To* A, "Put little dots here in white." (23)
A does white, **M** *does yellow of* (22). *A puts in white dots down left side, up right, and across top* (23). *M cuts off frayed end of feather and beats it to make it flexible.* M *does* (24).

M *To* A, "Put dots on the other side too." A *does* (26).

M *Remarks to me of* A's *work,* "Good!" M *does* (25).

M *To* A, "Yes like that." M *does* (27), *then* (28).

A "Shall I put dots here?" (26, 1 and 2)

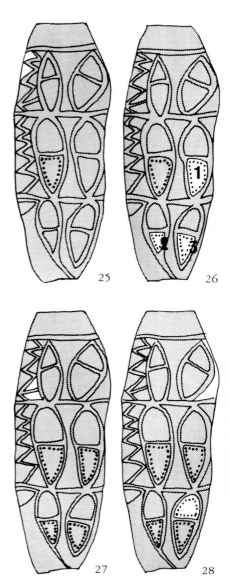

25   26

27   28

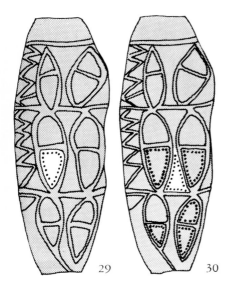

29   30

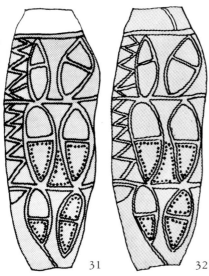

31   32

M "Yes, altogether. Mmm. No, in here?" (30)
A *started* (29), *now does* (30).

M "Do it all like that."
M *finishes* (28) *and stands off and looks at it.*

M "It's fine, excellent, fine!" *Cheers!*

A *still doing* (30). M *takes the stone palette and comes and squats at head of* bāg (31). M *puts in lines in head space* (32, 33, 34). A *finishes* (30), *jumps up, stands off, smiles joyfully at his work and runs off.* M *does* (35, 36, 37). A *returns.*

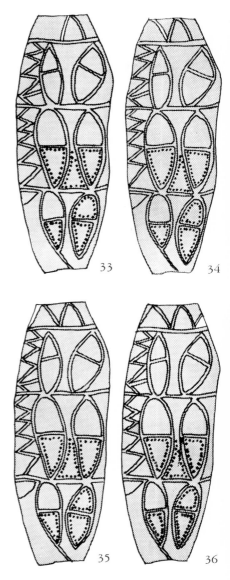

33

34

35

36

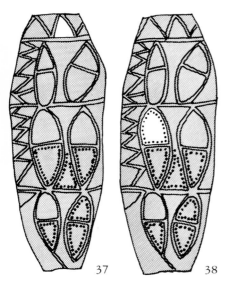

37   38

A   "Now what shall I do?"

M   "Put dots here." (38)
A *does* (38) *finishing what he had started before* (29) *but which* **M** *had rejected.* **M** *does* (39) *in red.* **M** *breaks a bit of bamboo from thatch fastening and tries as a brush. Rejects it and goes off. Re-*

39   40

turns *with a little piece of coconut leaf rib. Breaks it a little at end with hand.* A *at* M's *order now does* (40). M *moves his palette to top of* bāg *and mixes more red paint. With coconut brush* A *does* (42). *Then does* (43) *yellow.* A *does* (44) *without asking.*

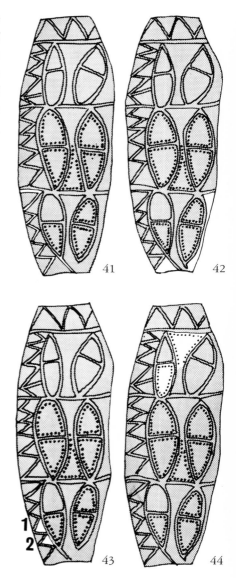

41

42

43

44

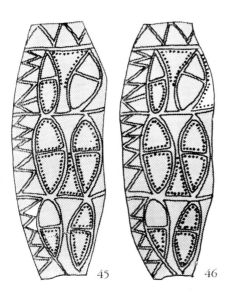

45   46

M   "Do dots here too." (46)
   M *finishes* (45) *and goes off leaving* A *to put in dots, three and a half hours since* M *marked off decorative fields.* M *returns and does* (47), *then* (48). *Lights his pipe.* A *does dots* (49). *Go on dotting.*

47   48

M *stretches and looks at it. Then does dots in head band.*

M "Next I'll make a snake." *Sits and stares. Does black edges in upper band while* A *does in grey.*

M "That's enough of that."

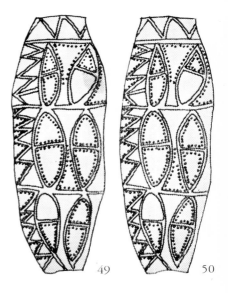

49   50

51

Junius B. Bird

TECHNOLOGY AND ART IN PERUVIAN TEXTILES

It is obvious that textiles provide an excellent ground for studying the relationship between technology and art. The interconnections are most evident in those fabrics where the desired results — the concepts of the artist — are achieved by structural means inherent in and inseparable from the craft itself, and where careful planning is required before and during construction. All of the many and varied ways in which fabrics can be created pose distinct technical problems. Each in some degree influences, limits, or controls the end result. Each technique is a medium in itself, providing a challenge to the ingenuity, imagination, and skill of the artist. What is more, the effects on style and on expression may extend beyond textiles and influence the styles of other media where similar controls do not exist.

There are other important divisions of textile art that can be termed non-structural and super-structural. Non-structural techniques include the varied procedures of applying dyes and pigments, free-hand painting, printing and stamping, resist dying, and the like. In all of them, the artist is completely free of structural restrictions. In fact, within this category, when the textile becomes nothing more than a base on which to express concepts, we are beyond the limits of textile art. This limit, however, is often difficult or impossible to determine. Function may provide a clue, yet even this is not a satisfactory basis for decision.

The super-structural techniques include anything added to a completed base fabric, such as embroidery or the appliqué of various materials. Again, there is freedom from structure unless, by choice, the work is deliberately interrelated to structure. Needlepoint and certain other embroidery are examples in which the structural relationship to the base fabric is chosen by the maker.

Our inquiry could easily be developed on a world-wide basis, irrespective of culture or period, but I believe the important facts can more easily be demonstrated by concentrating on the products of a single region, specifically Peru. One of the reasons prompting this choice is the fact that Peruvian fabrics furnish us with a sequence of structural design spanning approximately forty-five hundred years. This is a longer record than is yet available from any other region of the world. The material is abundant and, within it, we find manifold variations of nearly all textile techniques. Much, if not all, of it was produced on a family craft basis, largely for use by the makers. It is also note-worthy that textiles are the oldest known examples of Peruvian art and that long before the appearance of ceramics, or the working of metals, wood, and stone — all media employed extensively in later times Peru had a developed craft and tradi-tion of textile art.

At present we do not know if the first textiles originated entirely within Peru, or were imported from elsewhere. Certain trends or shifts that occur later seem to denote influence from other areas, but these are sporadic and infrequent. To a larger extent the changes in style, subject matter, and the development of, or emphasis on, different techniques mark the effects of rela-tive geographic and cultural isolation of areas within Peru, much of whose art exhibits regional trends and local variations. While these distinctions may be imperfectly known and docu-mented, this fact does not interfere with our immediate objec-tive of checking the relationship of technology and art within the textile field.

It should be pointed out, or at least admitted, that I am writing as an archaeologist, untrained in art history and only superficially familiar with similar studies. This being the case, we may avoid misunderstanding if I clarify my own conception of "art," it being a term that means different things to different people.

To me, art is exemplified by the Punuk, Ipiutak and Old Bering Sea Eskimos who were not content to produce merely efficient, functional tools, weapons and equipment, but spent much effort and time adding decorative features and details to make their possessions attractive. I have worked in the arctic and sub-arctic areas and have great respect for those early Eskimos who not only had the energy and stamina to survive under often adverse conditions, but had the imagination and initiative to encompass in everyday living more than the bare essentials of life, more than was needed to meet the requirements of food and shelter. One may argue correctly that we cannot interpret their motives, that they may have felt that their carvings had magical value and were for that reason essential. Perhaps so, but from what I have seen of their descendants I doubt that this was the only incentive.

With such a clue, you will not be surprised if I define art as something we could live without, yet do not choose to do so: it is a thing of the spirit, prompted by varied motives among which the desire for beauty and the satisfaction of creative work seem both ancient and widespread. Perhaps more attention should be paid to the motivation behind art, for conceivably the dividing line between primitive and non-primitive art could be drawn on a basis of motives, if these could be clearly defined. This naturally would be difficult, for a web of interrelated factors leads in diverse directions, far afield from our topic. However, I would like to mention one factor which, though it has little to do with the distinctions between primitive and non-primitive art, does exist; the compulsion people have to copy one another.

The Eskimo were and are as prone to plagiarism as our automobile designers. The people in one Eskimo community or area will copy one another in every detail of their dress, their kayaks, and their hunting and other equipment. This creates a problem. How can one distinguish between the motives inspiring the innovator or true artist and the quite different impulse of the artist's associates? As an archaeologist I cannot take a series of

Old Bering Sea harpoon points and distinguish the work of the innovator from the copies of his neighbors. We can accept them all as objects of art and among them distinguish the work of the beginner, the less gifted, the careless, and the skilled. Given a large enough series, we might, with perceptive study and analysis, identify the work of certain individuals. We can also plot the trends and changes which mark the passing of time and the regional differences, but little else.

A quite comparable situation exists for textiles. We could live comfortably if all fabrics were monochrome and no one had ever devised structural or other means of modifying appearance. However, the makers of textiles have not been content to do only this and for thousands of years have used fabrics for artistic expression. If you are reluctant to admit that many textiles are works of art, remember that I am inclined to class as art all that results from the effort to make things more than simply functional. The recognition of art in textiles is perhaps obscured by the great volume of past and present production. The work of the innovators and real artists is lost in the production of copyists, and our perception is perhaps numbed by the volume of the material to be considered. We tend to ignore the many ways weavers have devised to break the monotony of plain surface, by varying texture or appearance, by shifting construction technique, or by changing the materials, colors, and yarn twists. Such effects are a kind of non-objective art, which is an old, old story to weavers.

Before I illustrate with specific examples, let us first review a few basic facts about textiles, minimizing references to surface treatment after a fabric has been created and emphasizing those with structural features.

As you know, not all fabrics are woven; many can be classed as single element constructions, made either of one continuous yarn or cord, or of several used successively. A familiar example is knitting, the interlocking of one loop with another. Crocheting is another. In the same category are those fabrics in which the yarn end is passed through a succession of previously created loops — possibly the most ancient fabric-making technique used by man. Some have termed this "knotless netting" to distinguish it from related fabrics where, as in fish nets, knots fix the points of juncture.

When various elements or yarns are used in fabric construction, we can make two major divisions. One has a single set of elements which turn against each other, as in braiding or plaiting. The second has two sets of elements, the warp and weft, one sustaining the other. Both woven and twined products fall in this category and each may be elaborated by the addition of supplementary warp or weft or regionally inserted yarns.

What happens when the makers of these various fabrics are not content with a simple monochrome product or one in which the basic movements do not change? To what extent can the makers' concepts be freely expressed or to what extent are they limited or influenced by the techniques employed? These are the questions we are concerned with and will try to answer.

In all categories the simplest procedure to achieve variation or simple patterning is to substitute, or alternate, yarns of different colors, materials, size or twist. The result is banding or striping with effects which may range from the casual to the bold, the complex and extremely subtle. As examples occur throughout the full time range of Peruvian production, and because this is such a simple procedure, there is little point in detailed discussion. In passing, it is worth pointing out that when precise results are desired it is necessary to count the number of yarns or yarn turns in each unit. This has been done from earliest times to the present day. The same is true in more complex structural products. It thus seems possible that counting, beyond the minimal figures used by non-fabric-producing primitive peoples, developed as a result of early artists' efforts in the textile field.

Single Element Construction

Among the oldest known Peruvian fabrics of the preceramic stage, the commonest single element construction after fishnets is what can be called Figure 8 looping. The technique was widely distributed at the time, and in the Chicama valley constituted nearly 10 per cent of total production. After the introduction of pottery, its popularity in the Peruvian coastal area diminished and at an undetermined time ceased altogether. Today, bags in this technique are still made by tribes in the Montaña area of eastern Peru. Decoration of the modern example, when attempted, is limited to rudimentary color stripes even among groups who have an elaborate art style and a tradition of decorating many of their artifacts.

Among the ancient specimens, if color was applied, it has almost entirely disappeared and we can make no positive comment on its use. We do find, however, structural patterning at almost maximum development within the limits of the technique. This was achieved before 1500 B.C. and nothing comparable is known from any other region of the world where the technique persists.

Patterning and texture changes are accomplished by varying the lengths of the loops and their manner of interlacing. As it *plate 5* is impossible to create straight vertical or horizontal lines with these systems, pattern is based on diagonal lines or rows of openwork, generally on a grid plan. The angles of the diagonals are fixed by the width and length of the individual stitches or loops.

The products created may seem too simple to serve as examples of art. They are included to demonstrate that structural patterning is rigidly prescribed; that subtle textural differences were appreciated and were achieved with considerable effort, and that this appreciation appears at an early date. Also, what is true of the structural patterning of Figure 8 looping applies to allied single element constructions and to knotted

Plate 5. *A cotton fabric made of a single yarn in a succession of interlocked figure 8 loops. Variations of loop length, and manner of interlocking produce diagonal openwork grids and textural differences. Preceramic period. Chicama valley, Peru. American Museum of Natural History, New York.*

netting. Dull comments on them can be omitted.

plate 6   In later times, possibly in the second or third century B.C., a simpler form of looping was used to create men's shirts on which large, bold figures or geometric designs appear. These are made by color contrasts, not structural changes, and are of

Plate 6. A poncho-shirt of single element construction made with a threaded needle in rows of interlocked stitches. The angular nature of the motif reflects the structural limitations. Paracas culture. The Cleveland Museum of Art, gift of Mrs. R. Henry Norweb

necessity restricted to combinations of straight horizontal and diagonal lines. Again the angles are controlled by the proportions of individual loops, and the effect of curve, as in the chin line of the illustrated specimen, is only an illusion. In the manufacture of such pieces the artist builds up the figures transversely, row by row, starting at either end. Lacking paper on which the subject might be planned, he worked from a mental image when he was not copying what someone else had created. If errors or mistakes in composition occur, some can be compensated for by modification of total length.

It has been mentioned that knitting is basically a single element construction; that it is produced by pulling one loop through another. The technique was introduced into Peru by the Spaniards in the 16th century, was appreciated, and has been in continuous use ever since. One feature about knitting which we normally overlook is that any of it can be made backwards by using a threaded needle and creating stitches with the yarn end. The point where a knitter terminates a fabric is the starting point if we work with the threaded needle. It is the hard way, tedious and time consuming, yet around 2000 years ago some Peruvians discovered that it could be done. Working in this fashion, they added this reverse knitting to the surface or margins of a woven fabric as a kind of embroidery or super-*plate 7* structural detail. Using the same stitch, they also produced tubular straps or belts for use as turbans in which figures and motifs appear. Yarns of different colors were employed in succession and were carried forward or floated on the reverse or interior surface. As in ordinary knitting, all figures are composed of vertical, horizontal, and balanced diagonal lines.

Plate 7. Tubular turban strap structurally identical with knitting. The design is definitely limited by the technique. Paracas culture. The Textile Museum, Washington, D. C.

Plate 8. Paracas embroidery, reproducing the angular nature of figures created in the more restrictive technique shown in Plate 7. Detail from a mantle presented to the United Nations by the Peruvian government

Any appearance of curve is actually a combination of angles. The result is an angular treatment of subject matter, a forced stylization from which there is no escape.

The production of reverse knitting needlework turban straps by the Paracas people of Peru had an influence worth noting in connection with our topic. At the time, current fashion in clothing called for the use of costume in which all articles worn at one time matched in color combinations and sequence, and repeated the same motifs. The most favored medium was embroidery with complex application of colors and a large inventory of motifs. As remarked, embroidery provides freedom of expression, but this was sacrificed when a gentleman acquired one of the new turban straps. To be in fashion and

plate 8   have his other garments match the turban, the embroidery had to follow or reproduce the limitations of the technique employed in the turban. We do not have an inventory of the clothing found with every individual of the time, but if we did, I believe we would find that such representation in embroidery became popular in its own right. This is only surmise,

plate 9   prompted by the frequency of occurrence of embroidered articles in the style, a frequency out of proportion to the number of strap turbans in collections.

It is neither possible nor necessary to include all fabric techniques in this review. We can skip plaiting, noting only that elaborate and beautiful products were created in Peru. Loom

plate 10   plaiting, sometimes referred to by the Swedish term "spräng," appeared in the late preceramic period. It is a technique widely and anciently distributed in the world and still used to some extent, though nowhere in as complex a manner as in certain late

Plate 9. Detail from the neck of a Paracas embroidered shirt, contemporary with that of Plate 8, which although it was made with the same stitch, lacks the angular quality. Museo Nacional de Antropologia y Arqueologia, Lima

56

Plate 10. Loom plaited ornamental tabs, one of the most complex developments of the system ever achieved. The unfinished sections which connected the yarn during construction are covered with needle work when cut apart. Nazca culture. The Textile Museum, Washington, D.C.

Nazca products of about 500 to 650 A.D. Some of these had six sets of warp of three contrasting colors interchanged to create patterns and figures while six layers of fabric were being formed. The great skill and patience required must have made the products highly prized, and it will not be surprising if we find a comparable interrelationship between techniques and design as remarked in the case of the Paracas turbans.

Fabrics with Two Sets of Elements: Twining and Weaving

Motifs and patterns can be created in twining and weaving with either the warp or weft yarns, or by an interplay of both. In twining, wefts are handled in pairs and encircle or twine about the warps, in contrast to the interlacing of warp and weft in weaving. There are no mechanical aids which will simplify the work of twining; each twist of the weft is a separate finger manipulation. With weaving, heddle controls greatly simplify the basic process. Both techniques are present among the oldest known preceramic fabrics, but twining was much more commonly employed, possibly because heddle controls for weaving were not known.

All of the ancient twined fabrics have the weft rows spaced, not compacted together, except in end finishes or, rarely, as narrow bands. This means that more warp than weft is visible and that striped effects are much more apparent when done with the

Plate 11. Menomini twined bag, showing figures created by a warp manipulation system used in the preceramic period of Peru. Motifs are combinations of horizontal, vertical and diagonal lines. Color distribution is reversed on opposite side. American Museum of Natural History, New York

warp than the weft. Structural patterns involving the use of colors were accomplished by warp manipulations, the shifting or transposing of warps from their normal parallel positions in order to concentrate color where desired on either one face or the other. Two allied systems of manipulation were used; one unreported from any other part of the world; the other used by the Woodland Indian tribes of North America. In both systems the wefts simply hold the warps in place and do not form any part of the figures or patterns.

In the preceramic examples available for study, color has faded and largely disappeared. Figures must be reconstructed by plotting the yarn movements with the aid of a microscope. Unfortunately lacking a Peruvian specimen with a complete motif in the Woodland type technique, a Menomini bag made about 1900 is shown. The motif is necessarily angular, was constructed row by row, working from the bottom towards the top. We do not know whether an older example served as a model or whether the

plate 11

Plate 12. Section of a Peruvian, warp patterned, twined fabric circa 2000 B.C. Construction and design limitations are similar to the twined fabric of Plate 11, but color was more concentrated. Retouched photograph. American Museum of Natural History, New York

60

maker worked only from a mental image. Certainly there is a considerable repetition of motifs in Menomini twined fabrics, so presumably these were traditional.

The second twined patterning system produces more solid *plate 12* concentration of color. In both systems color shifts occur at the line of the weft, so straight, sharp color breaks can be created along this line. As the warps slant between weft rows, all break in color along the line of the warp is inevitably wavy. With the Woodlands type, straight-line diagonals are possible; with the other, the diagonals are serrated or stepped. The result is that there will be a marked difference in the appearance of a figure or motif, depending on its orientation in relation to warp or weft. The artist working with these twining systems must take this difference into consideration and must plan accordingly.

One might assume that the effect of the limitations of such a technique would have little influence once alternate textile procedures were available or developed. This was not necessarily so. One of the preceramic period motifs, a double headed snake-like *plate 13* figure, survived with some popularity for over 3000 years. In the twined version the jagged body lines are a result of the normal *plate 14* warp movement along a diagonal. The effect became part of the concept, and we find that for many centuries after twining was no longer used, this serration was accentuated when creating the *plate 15* figures by other less restrictive methods.

The presence of weaving in the preceramic period has been mentioned. Here again structural patterning is limited to warp manipulation, the floating of sections of the warps at desired *plate 16* points. Such warp patterning persisted throughout the subsequent textile record and is today the principal textile art form of *plate 17* the Highland Indians of southern Peru and Bolivia. As is true in all structurally patterned woven fabrics, coarse yarns and low *plate 18* yarn counts accentuate the geometric appearance of figures, an effect reduced but not eliminated by the use of fine yarns and high counts.

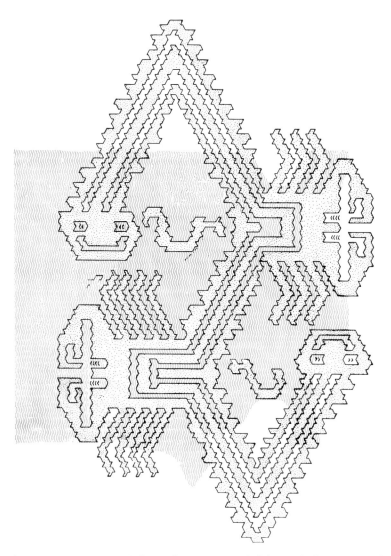

Plate 13. *Reconstructed figure from a twined fabric of the preceramic period, showing rock crabs appended to a double headed snake. In this example about 5000 separate finger manipulations create the figure; over 8000 the background. As shown, the warps run vertically. American Museum of Natural History, New York*

Plate 14. Reconstructed bird figures in a Peruvian twined fabric made prior to 2000 B.C. As shown the warps run horizontally. American Museum of Natural History, New York

Plate 15. An example of a double headed snake in a weft pattern. Although made probably in the 15th century A.D., some 3000 years after the one shown in Plate 13, it retains the concept of serrated margins, a necessary structural feature of the early version. Central Coast. American Museum of Natural History, New York

Plate 16. Woven fabric with stylized bird figures created by warp floats. Circa 1600 B.C. in the Peruvian preceramic period. American Museum of Natural History, New York

Plate 17. Warp patterned double headed snake. Ocoña, Acari valley area, 15th to 16th centuries. The Textile Museum, Washington, D.C.

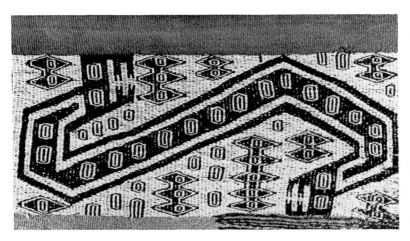

Plate 18. Bottom: Modern warp pattern belt made about 1955 by a high-land weaver near Huancayo, Peru. Top: Navajo tapestry circa 1875 show-ing a similar subject in an unrelated technique, one capable of far more realism than the warp pattern below. Collection Dr. Junius B. Bird, New York

Tapestry, which is the complete opposite of warp patterning, appears first in Peru in the Chavin horizon, perhaps about 900 B.C. It is a technique which can be used to achieve a high degree of realism or almost any presentation an artist-weaver may wish. Among Peruvian fabrics there are thousands of examples, some more finely executed than any contemporary European products. At times it became very popular, and complex figures and designs were created, yet not until the 16th century, under the influence and encouragement of the Spanish, was there any departure from a rather rigid, stylized treatment of subject matter. One is led to suspect that tapestry design was strongly influenced by what was produced in more prescribed textile techniques. In a sense the

plate 19

plate 20

plate 21

plate 22

situation may parallel the similarity one finds between the double cloth figure and the painted mummy "mask" from the same area

plates 23, 24 and period. The nature of the woven figure is set by the technique, while the painting shows similar treatment without being an attempt at copying.

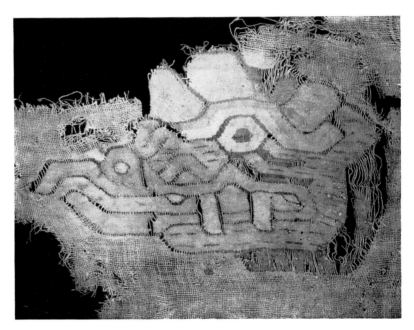

Plate 19. An early example of the use of tapestry in Peru, a condor head with feline fangs created in a plain weave field, part of an elaborate art style which focused on mystical themes. Chavin period, Supe. American Museum of Natural History, New York

*Plate 20. Tapestry detail, 2¾ inches high, from a miniature shirt of the
Tiahuanaco period. Technically an extremely fine product, made by a
highly skilled weaver at a time when tapestry achieved great popularity.
Mr. and Mrs. A. B. Martin, Guennol Collection, on loan to the Brooklyn
Museum*

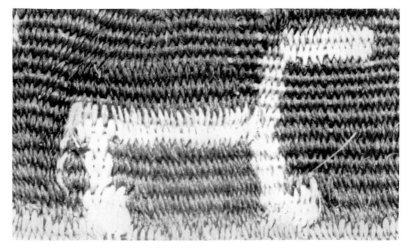

Plate 21. *Llama figure, 9 millimeters long, a detail of an Inca period tapestry, areas of which have weft yarns at the rate of 500 per inch. Inca weavers never utilized the full artistic possibilities of their techniques. Collection Rafael Larco Hoyle, Lima*

Plate 22. *Detail of a colonial Peruvian tapestry made in the late 16th or early 17th centuries, by descendants of Inca weavers who preserved the native technical skills yet were influenced by European concepts. Museum of the American Indian, Heye Foundation, New York*

Plate 23. Mythical figure in double cloth of the Paracas culture, possibly 2nd or 3rd centuries B.C. A fully mastered medium, the style results from acceptance of technical limitations with no effort made to soften or modify them. The Textile Museum, Washington, D.C.

70

Double cloth is a fabric in which two sets of warps and wefts   *plate 23* create two layers of fabric. Angular figures and patterns result from alternating the positions of sections of the fabric as they are woven. We do not know when this was first attempted in Peru. The specimen illustrated was probably made several centuries B.C. and as it shows full mastery of the method, older examples should be found. Later, the use of double cloth was widespread and common, so the problems of design were well understood.

Another quite distinct technique is gauze, in which warps are   *plate 25*

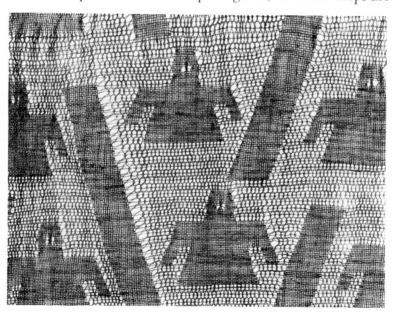

Plate 25. *Figures in plain weave in a gauze movement field, a medium with very rigid limits. Late Paracas culture, possibly beginning of the Christian era. The Textile Museum, Washington, D.C.*

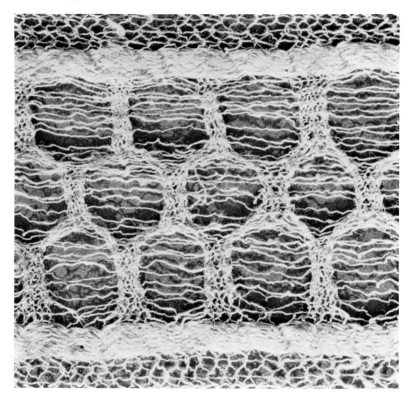

transposed and held out of parallel by the weft. Patterning is accomplished by alternating areas of plain weave or by varying the transposition movements. In most cases the products are monochrome. If more than one color is used, they run as stripes, independent of any figure or pattern. As there is a close analogy between the warp movements in gauze and some of the twined fabrics, it is surprising that it does not occur in the preceramic material. The oldest examples are in the Chavin horizon, and *plate 26* from then on it was widely used.

In contrast to double cloth, the nature of gauze designs, unless on a large bold scale, are much more restricted. Except with transmitted light, they are in general visually unimpressive and at a short distance some can be virtually invisible. This fact lends interest, for the gauzes illustrate the willingness of Peruvian weavers to work with a subtle medium in which there are many problems for the designer.

Mention has been made of the fact that the Peruvians had no paper to aid in design planning. Starting in the first centuries

A.D., needle worked samplers were used. The oldest are guides for embroidered figures while later ones could have helped in planning structural products. They are rare in collections but could have been rather commonly used. Late period tombs in and near the Chancay valley have yielded a number of small looms, often with unfinished fabrics. At first these appear as normal samplers, showing assemblages of motifs and patterns often in several techniques. The fact that the majority are unfinished, that the loom parts are often crude makeshifts, suggests that they were made just as grave offerings, possibly to provide the departed with reference for favored themes.

plate 27

plate 28

Within a short review, we cannot comment on all the varied aspects of textile art. The examples chosen should make our point: that technique limits and affects the work of the artist. One question remains: does technique lead to the independent development of the same motif? Personally I doubt that this is

Plate 29. Inca style poncho-shirt of tapestry, probably post-Conquest, with one form of the eight pointed star, the most widely distributed textile motif in the world. The Textile Museum, Washington, D.C.

so, for the simple reason that the most widely distributed textile motif in the world does not appear in Peru during 4000 years of textile production.

The motif referred to is the simple eight-pointed star which appears *ad nauseum* in textiles the world over. The reason for

plate 29

Plate 30. *Other versions of the eight pointed star, from the Great Lakes region: A. Potawatomi Indian twined weft pattern, and B. Winnibago Indian beaded bag; C. Weft pattern from Formosa. American Museum of Natural History, New York*

its wide use is simply that it can be created in any technique which will permit the formation of vertical, horizontal, and balanced diagonal lines. Any novice weaver or knitter can produce it, and it unfortunately lends itself to mass production on mechanical looms. I do not know its early record, but it was introduced into Spain by the Moors, was in common use at the time of the Spanish conquests in America, and survives there today. In America we find it in historic and modern native prod- *plate 30* ucts, from some twined Woodland bags in the United States, down through Mexico, Central and South America, to the Auricanians of Chile and the weavers of the Argentine. Among archaeological fabrics of Peru, it is limited to specimens most of which are clearly post-Conquest. The only possible exceptions are a few examples which a qualified observer states are immediately pre-Spanish. This, however, does not refute the fact that there is no trace of the figure in the products of many thousands of weavers for approximately 4000 years. Also, that once accepted there is no relief from it; witness the post-Conquest record.

The conclusion is obvious. While technical limitations will give a common character to products in any one technique, these do not necessarily lead to the development of similar or identical motifs. They do seem to encourage the persistence of repetition of themes and to favor long-term continuity — features which merit further study.

Hans Himmelheber

PERSONALITY AND TECHNIQUE
OF AFRICAN SCULPTORS

Sculpture plays only a minor role among the artistic activities of the Africans. Whereas singing and dancing are ever present, sculpture does not even exist among all tribes. It is almost non-existent in eastern and southern Africa. In west and central Africa we find tribes who do not carve at all, right among others who excel in it, such as the artistically sterile Agni tribes of the eastern Ivory Coast, side by side with their most creative cousins, the Baule; or the Kru tribe, Guere, with so many masks and fine metal castings, next to their relatives, the Bassa, who do not carve at all.

The reason does not lie in a difference of institutions or beliefs, which are always akin among related tribes. But carvings are not *necessary*. Instead of using a wooden mask, you may take a piece of cloth in which you cut holes for eyes and mouth; instead of a wooden ancestor figure you may form some crude symbol of clay.

To further explain this difference of artistic activity from tribe to tribe, we must know that the carving in a tribe depends on only a few artists. To introduce carving in a tribe it may suffice for one individual to learn it from a carver in a neighboring tribe, and to have three or four apprentices in the following years. I know a large region in Liberia and the Ivory Coast inhabited by two different tribes whose many carvings are practically all made by one artist and his disciples. In the same way, carving may disappear from a region if by some coincidence the few artists there die. This happened among the Minianka who carved some of the beautiful antelopes (tji wara) of the Bambara.

Tasks of the Carver

For the African this world is twofold: the visible world of men, and the invisible world of the spirits. The spirits have a desire to be materialized; or, rather, to have a material representation in this material world. To achieve this, a spirit appears to a human being in a dream or vision. It urges the man or woman to accept it, to furnish it with a material representation. This may be a mask, or a figure, or a mixture of certain herbs and charcoal in an antelope horn. The spirit will then serve the person, who in turn will feed the spirit with sacrifices and will keep certain taboos. The spirit does not permanently reside in this object; the object is only the spirit's way of making itself known to humans so that they can communicate with it.

Masks: Nearly all African tribes who practice carving have masks, and some tribes have no other carvings than masks. A mask is always connected with a certain spirit. The entire apparition is supposed to be a superhuman being coming from the bush, and that is why it wears a raffia skirt. In most cases the mask has also the traits of a human being, but to indicate that it is a creature from the bush the artist often adds certain characteristics of animals, notably horns, teeth, a big mouth. And again, there are animal masks, notably of strong animals like the elephant, chimpanzee, or buffalo. Sometimes parts of different animals are united in one mask, this depending upon the indications the spirit gave to the man to whom it first revealed itself in a dream. If human, the mask is often distinctly male or female, carrying a woman's headdress or a man's beard. Yet among the Dan, and probably other tribes, it is addressed with the pronoun "it", not "he" or "she", to indicate that it is not a human being.

The mask has several aspects, but the main characteristic of a mask is its sanctity. Even as a spirit's material manifestation, a mask cannot use force; but it must be respected. Based on this, masks are used by many tribes to guard the boys in the initiation bush against the evil influences of people with witchcraft. For instance, all the masks of the Bayaka but two, and most of the masks of the Badjokwe in the Congo, are initiation-camp masks.

A second widespread function of the masks is to keep law and order within the chiefdom. In many African tribes the chiefs do not have an armed force to keep peace among the subjects, or to enforce an action in the public interest. The spirits, through the masks, take care of that. There we observe the mask's untouchability at its highest degree. The peacemaking mask may sit down between the fighting parties, raise its hand and command peace. None would then dare to lift his spear again. These same masks see to it that the traditional laws are kept — the village taboos, for instance — and they may proclaim new laws, such as a regulation that all members of the group shall be free to take a certain amount of food from anybody's field when traveling.

Thirdly, masks are used for mere entertainment. It is certainly not correct to assume that all these entertaining masks are sunk down from higher significance in former times. The entertaining function, when we witness it, proves to be deeply rooted in native life. Masks of this kind are of two opposing categories, showing the old dualism of the good and the mischievous spirits. The good ones dance, sing the history of the town or of the chief's deeds, or appear when good news has reached the town. The negative ones, so to speak, set the town on fire. Such masks chase everybody around in a nasty way, and that's what they are expected to do.

These then are the three main functions of the masks: protection during the circumcision or initiation time, maintaining of social order, and entertainment in a positive and a negative sense. There are more functions, to be sure. We see the masks at sowing and harvesting time with the Guro and Bambara. The Dan have war masks which actually lead the men to war, accompanied by their musicians. When we see a mask attend a certain event, however, we cannot be sure that this is the mask's real function. The mask may just appear there to raise the importance of the occasion. We sometimes find the designation "funeral mask": now, the masks appearing at the funerals of the Senufo, for example, are merely delegated there by the Lo Society, to which most Senufo of the farmers' and the blacksmiths' caste belong, to honour the deceased dignitary. Their real functions are nevertheless those of protection during the initiation period.

Figures: Second in importance among the tasks of the African carver are human figures. Easiest for us to understand is the ancestor figure. Among the Senufo, the patriarch of a family would lead me through two or three chambers of his mud house into the ancestor rooms. In the first one hung the tails of the family's dead horses. In the second one stood two wooden figures, male and female, in the light ray which fell down through a skylight. These were the family's ancestor figures. Beside them lay several other figures, the servants of the ancestors, who had accompanied the old people into the realm of the dead. The ancestor figure is *not* the permanent abode of the spirit. It is not correct to say that the spirit is deceived by the figure, or caught by it, to keep it from doing harm to the survivors. The figure is rather, as one Dan put it, the *channel* through which one can speak to the ancestor.

Other figures represent other spirits. Among the Basonge, for example, a spirit will appear to a man in a dream and ask to have a figure carved for it by a carver. The man will then be its priest. The spirit will henceforward assist the man's community in all troubles. As the years go by it becomes evident that in many cases the spirit did *not* help, so confidence in it decreases. Then a new spirit will soon appear to a man in his dream, offer its services and ask for a figure to be carved for it. Thus we find a continual coming and dying of these figures. We must know that the carver, for all the spiritual importance of his masks and figures, is not *himself* a priest, medicine man or sorcerer. He is a carver, and that is all.

Applied art: Some tribes also have an important production of applied art. They decorate their spoons, combs, and handles of flybrushes or swords, with geometrical designs or with little animals or human faces. There are tribes like the Bakuba in the Congo who have an abundance of applied art, but almost no masks and figures. We note in passing that ornamental design in Africa is almost purely geometric, and always symmetrical. Sometimes an animal is carved into the ornament, but only one which is looked upon from above, so that it will appear symmetrical to the eye: a scorpion, a spider, a crocodile. Motives of plants seem to be lacking in African art at first sight, if we except old Benin art. However, my son has recently found that some of the geometrical designs on pots are based on plant motives.

The artists

Women do not carve. Nearly all African handicrafts are exercised by either men *or* women, but carving is men's trade. Women *could* show their talent in plastic art in pottery. Pottery is women's trade all over Africa. Yet African women never try to form anything but simple pots. They don't even knead some animal for their child to play with when they form the little sausages out of which they will build the pot. I know of only one exception, among the Bamessing and Bamesi in the Cameroon Grassland.

Artisans and artists: I used to start my interviews with the carvers with the question: "How was it that you became a carver?" Among some tribes, for example, the Baule, the carver mostly gave a practical reason. "Really," he might say, "I did not want to become a carver. I would have preferred to become a weaver. But since my uncle was a carver and was willing to teach me for nothing, my father ordered me to learn this trade." Another one said: "I wanted to get married, but I was not good-looking, so I desired to learn some trade which would give me a certain importance." If I continued to ask one of these men what induced him to sit down and carve, he usually answered: "I carve if I receive an order from someone."

"Do you prefer to carve or to go farming?" The answer: "Carving is hard work. I even prefer bush-cutting to carving.

84

For when cutting the bush I may pause once in a while to talk to the girls, whilst in carving I have to think all the time whether I should proceed this way or that way."

Among such tribes, then, the carver as a rule is more an artisan than an artist. There are exceptions, of course.

We now proceed to some other tribe, say to the Badjokwe in the Congo and Angola. Here the carvers are more artists in the sense which we give to this word. If I asked a man here how it was that he became a carver, I was frequently told that he began when he was a child. "I used to go into the bush to look for some soapstone or the tuberous root of wild yam. From it, I tried to carve the faces of my friends. One day, when I brought some such carving into town, people said: 'Why, this looks like little Maliboka.' That made me realize that I could become a carver."

One young carver among the Dan told me that during his apprenticeship he and his brother were so eager to learn carving that when their father called them home to help him in farming they used the first opportunity to run away and return to their carving. One apprentice among the Kran, who was not really wanted by his master, patiently kept on just cutting trees for the master's carving for a long time, until one day the master took pity on him and let him start carving.

These artists tell us that they do not wait for people to order objects. "Sometimes my heart becomes restless. It tells me to get busy with some good carving. I then take my tools and retire to my secret place of work in the bush. As I carve some fine object there, my heart will sit down again." The carvers of these tribes, then, are true artists as we know them, artists who create their works because they feel an urge to do so. I do not mean to say that all artists of one tribe are either *artisans* or *artists,* but only that according to my experience the tendency in *some* tribes seems to be markedly this way, with others the other way.

Heritage: Carving, like all special occupations, often passes on from father to son through many generations. This is partly due to the African's belief that a man's fundamental gifts are left to his successor at his death. Among the Dan and Kran, when the dead body of the master is laid out, the man who is entitled to obtain his gifts steps four times across the corpse, at the same time bowing down to it and moving his arms as if he were taking something from the dead man to place it on his own shoulders. "Give me your skill in carving," he will say. Naturally, the son is authorized to speak first if he so desires. Furthermore, the *tools* of the master are supposed to contain some of his skill. So they, too, are greatly valued by his successors. Carver Dru of the Kran was the favorite disciple of the greatest artist of this tribe. He sadly told me that another disciple of lower standing had somehow managed to inherit the tools and was therefore likely to surpass him in the future.

Carving linked to other occupations: Among some tribes, carving is linked to another occupation: with the Dogon of the western Sudan the carving of certain masks is entrusted to young men who do this, as Griaule reports, as part of their ritual function in a religious festival. We cannot expect them to be true artists then, nor even to be skilful artisans.

There are other tribes in the western Sudan with whom carving is part of the blacksmith's work. It is so among the Bambara. This is understandable, as the blacksmith *must* be a carver to some extent when he has to make appropriate handles for the bush knives and axes he manufactures.

Among the Dan and Kran, the blacksmith exerts some influence on the carvers. Because it is he who manufactures the carvers' tools, a gift is due him whenever one of the carvers of his town sells an object. For this same reason he even has authority over the men who perform with masks. He can temporarily take the mask from its owner, if this man has broken one of the mask taboos. Often the masks are kept in the smithy, up under the roof.

Carvers as a caste: Among the Senufo of the northern Ivory

Coast the carvers form a special caste. Like all the tribesmen of this region, the Senufo are subdivided into a number of castes according to their economic activity. Highest rank the farmers, who own the soil and provide food for the other castes. Second are the blacksmiths, who manufacture the tools without which the farmers could not cultivate their fields. Third in rank are the weavers. Last and least, as lowest of the castes, come the artists: the singers and the carvers. When I asked a Senufo of the farmers' caste whether he could marry a carver's daughter he turned away in disgust: "Such a one," he said, as if the carvers were hardly human beings.

The women of each caste also exercise some special trade. The blacksmiths' wives brew beer from millet and honey. The women of the carvers' and singers' families also exercise low ranking occupations: on market day we find the carvers' wives sitting apart, busily mending the calabashes of the higher ranking women for a few cowrie shells. The singers' wives, like our gypsy women, are fortune tellers. They also dance in public in a provocative way, as girls of a higher caste would never do.

These castes of the Senufo live in towns of their own, except the singers, who dwell with their noble masters, the farmers, whose praise they sing when guests arrive. Thus when we travel in Senufo country we always encounter not single towns, but a cluster of separated towns: a farmers' town, a blacksmiths' town, a weavers' town, a carvers' town. Carvers' towns, however, we do not find with all Senufo settlements, since there is much less demand for carvings than for blacksmiths' or weavers' products.

The carvers' towns of a vast territory of Senufo country I could finally trace back to one original town from which they all derived directly or indirectly. It is therefore likely that the carvers were originally one certain family, which perhaps had moved in from another tribe.

Among these Senufo, then, a carver is forced to be a carver by virtue of his birth. A child born in the carvers' caste *must* become a carver. No consideration is given to whether he is gifted or not. On the other hand, a child born in a different caste, say in the farmers', *cannot* become a carver even if he feels the urge to be one. At a workplace of Senufo carvers we see very young boys already taking part in their fathers' trade, carving little spoons and even small figures.

A Senufo carver remains anonymous his life long. If a person wishes to order some carving, he goes to the carvers' town and speaks to the chief about it. When he has gone, the chief passes the order on to the carver he thinks best fitted for the work in question. Consider what this must mean for a true artist. His inspiration, his efforts, his skill will not be rewarded by the applause of his public, for the public does not know him. All the stimulus which ambition furnishes to the artist does not become effective in Senufo art. We shall later see what it does mean to the artists of other tribes; yet Senufo art reaches the highest levels.

We keep in mind that these conditions of the artists among the tribes of the western Sudan and the Senufo are exceptional: that carving is linked to another occupation or to a carver's caste.

We now turn back to all the other carving tribes of west and central Africa. There the carvers are *free* to take up this profession.

Prestige: Among all these tribes of west and central Africa the carver enjoys high prestige. I know several chiefs who are proud of being carvers; one of them, a Dan, being at the same time also a blacksmith; and he can also make casts from brass. We even know of a former king of the great Bakuba tribe in the Congo who was a carver. In the Cameroons one carver was so highly respected for his skill and grew so rich through it, that upon the old chief's death his tribesmen elected him chief. With some tribes the carver, if he is an outstanding one, is given a title by his chief, comparable to the French "maître." Or he may carry a fancy axe over his shoulder as a sign of his highly valued occupation.

Plate 31. In the Congo a Bayaka artist paints the top of a mask according to an elder's instructions

Apprenticeship: A young man chooses his future profession *plates 31, 32* at an age between seventeen and twenty years, but sometimes I found even men of about thirty as apprentices in some trade.

The future carver usually passes an apprenticeship of two to three years' duration with a master. During this time he has to help his master in his farming.

Among some tribes, like the Kran and Dan, the apprentices do not remain permanently with the master in his village during their apprenticeship. They go to visit him whenever they feel like it, stay with him for a few days, start some carving under his supervision, and return home to finish it.

The master is paid for passing on his profitable knowledge. As a rule the fee is quite high. He finds even more profit in a custom which applies to all African professions: that the former pupil during all his lifetime will continue to bring gifts to his master. He does so not only because of personal attachment, but

Plate 32. An apprentice of a Guro carver in the Ivory Coast listens to the instructions of his master

because the master never ceases to be in a spiritual sense his superior. Without his sympathy the young carver cannot succeed in his work. If in a town there is just one old carver and several younger ones who have learned the art from him, the old man remains their boss as long as he lives. We, for instance, have to ask his permission and must dash him even if we only want to take pictures of one of the younger carvers. Yet among all the carvers I interviewed in so many different tribes, there were only a few who did not speak of their old master in terms of affection.

There is no methodical teaching. Usually the pupil does not

even begin with some easy task, to proceed gradually to more difficult ones. He learns *by imitation*. The master just carves what he wants to carve, and orders the apprentice to take a piece of wood and do as *he* does. This is surprising to us Westerners, who in teaching analyze our doings and teach them step by step. There is, however, this other way of teaching *by imitation* which does not pass by the intellect. Chinese calligraphers employ this same method of teaching by imitation.

One day the master will tell the apprentice that he is now an independent sculptor. There was, for instance, one apprentice among the Kran who stayed with his master in the residence of some chief for whom the master was carving. When the master had half finished a figure, another chief asked him to come and carve for him. The apprentice offered to stay and finish the figure. When the old master returned he found the figure perfectly done. "You are free now," he said to the young man. "Go back to your town and do your carving there. Then come and show me what you have carved."

The freed young carver nearly always returns to his own town, where he enjoys many advantages through his family links. He even does so if there are already other carvers there, for a carver's work is never urgent, and customers will not mind coming to him from other towns.

Sale of carvings: The sculptors do not offer their carvings in any way. They do not carry them to market, nor is there anything like our exhibitions of art. There are no dealers either, whereas for pottery we find them occasionally.

The customers may come from far away — even from other tribes. In a Baule town which specialized in certain carvings covered with gold leaf, I met envoys from a distant eastern Agni king who had ordered a kind of crown from these Baule.

A famous carver may be called by a chief to his residence, and stay there for a year or two to carve for the big man and his nobles.

If a carver has made some fine, extraordinary object out of his own imagination he will usually give it to his own chief for a present. "You see," they say, "we always tried to make our chief the wealthiest of all."

A mask or a figure is rather highly priced in relation to other African goods. Whereas earthen pots made by women cost only pennies, a mask may well cost two goats; and if it is a very important one, even a cow or a girl. The reason for this high valuation is not only the artist's rare skill, but also the importance of the object. Whenever an African obtains an object of a magical nature, he must *sacrifice* something. The harder the sacrifice, the greater will be the power of the object. That is why he is quite willing to pay a heavy price for his mask, for this will increase the importance of it.

Nevertheless, it is rare that a carver can live by his carving alone, as the blacksmiths often live by their ironwork. Most of the carvers exist, like everybody, mainly on their farming. So the sculptor does not carve day after day.

Artist to artist: The artist strives to attain fame. In an African community, much more than with us, every man and every woman wants to be important in some way. One man is the best hunter with traps, another one is head of a secret society; this woman is "mother of the fetishes," that one is the most hospitable of her quarter. So the artist's ambition is not out of the ordinary.

The sculptors are jealous of each other's successes. In one region in Liberia each of the two leading carvers told me independently that every fine piece of sculpture in this country was his work. If "another one" claimed that he had made one of these objects, that was a lie! One Baule carver, when taking on a new apprentice, kills a chicken for his fetish so that this boy may learn better than the apprentices of the other carvers.

Technique

The carvers usually know four or five different kinds of wood suited best for masks, spoons, figures or combs. For very fine masks they use certain extremely hard root wood, which will not be attacked by termites in the course of the years, and which becomes shiny when rubbed with oil.

After felling the tree, they usually start right off to work the wood. Wood in this green stage is easier to work, they say. It follows, however, that the carvings frequently crack as they dry. To forestall this, the carver rubs the finished objects thoroughly with palm oil, and repeats this procedure several times during the two weeks which follow. The oil fills the pores, causing the wood to dry slowly.

The carver uses very few tools. Most of them have only an adze and a small knife. Some also use a chisel and a hooked tool to hollow out spoons or the backside of masks. Sometimes one finds a peculiarity: A Bashilele carver has fastened his knife to a long handle; he presses the handle under his arm, thus lending the lever strength of his arm to his cutting whilst the fingers maneuver the knife.

To soften the surface a certain leaf is used, whose surface is so rough that it takes off irregularities like sandpaper.

The finished carving is always colored, though mostly only blackened. Certain leaves may be used which yield a black juice after being pounded in the mortar. The Bashilele carver burns resin and uses the thick black smoke to blacken a palm wine cup.

To obtain correct and agreeable dimensions for a mask, the artist may measure his own face with his fingers, or that of a pretty girl. He then usually starts to hew deep grooves across the block of wood to mark the place where the eyes will be between forehead and cheeks; the deepening between nose and mouth; and the one below the mouth. After that, he gives the mask its circumference, then hews out the two sides of the nose. From then onwards he works fairly evenly on all the traits. He carves only very shortly on one trait, then turns the object round and continues on another one. In between, but not often, he pauses to hold the object at arm's length to judge it. He then willingly accepts the advice of some elder master.

When carving the face of a male figure I saw the Bekalebue use this little trick: the lower two thirds of the block of wood was carved to form a protruding triangle. The point of the triangle was then carved into the nose. Under it, the two sides of the triangle indicated the two corners of the mouth, and the base was to be the beard.

A surprising peculiarity of the sculptor's technique, to be observed with all tribes, is that the carver's most important utensil is the little adze, which our own sculptors do not use at all. The heavy strong strokes of this instrument fall on the wood with absolute accuracy. All the traits of the face appear nearly finished before the artist lays the adze aside to use the knife. This unfailing skill in handling the adze seems a miracle again every time we witness it.

Among some tribes like the Dan the carvers work hard, from morning till evening, with just one break for eating. With them, it is surprising to observe how quickly the work progresses. A normal mask can well be finished in just one day, a large ladle in two. Among other tribes like the Baule the carvers prefer to take it easy, to carve for two or three hours, then turn to some other occupation, to continue the next day. My impression is that those carvers who are real artists are the more diligent ones, and stick to their work until it is finished because they are themselves eager to see their creation perfected.

Among all tribes, I met carvers who liked to carve several objects at a time, as perhaps four masks of different types. The Bayaka carver even works the set of five or seven or nine masks for the circumcision camp all at one time. He turns from one mask to another, and to the third and fourth and fifth and back again, thus working them fairly evenly.

The Ashanti and their cousins, the Baule, can cover their woodcarvings with gold leaf of their own production. They dig the gold from alluvial deposits, melt it into small lumps, and hammer these into gold leaf of paper thickness. The object to be gilded is densely ornamented, covered with beeswax or a paste of manioc flour, and the gold is pressed into the grooves of the ornaments with a little pointed ivory stick the size of a toothpick.

Clay Sculpture: Speaking of technique, I must at least mention that all over Africa there also exists sculpture in clay, of which I have not yet made a special study. The men who form these sculptures are not identical with the carvers. I have seen on the wall of a Baule house a clay figure formed by the owner of the house to commemorate his encounter with a certain fairy in the bush. Among these same Baule a medicine man by the name of Surobua builds little houses across the paths leading to the towns, and forms certain terrifying animals on the walls and in the chambers of the house, to guard the town. I have never met a man who, like the carvers, made clay sculptures professionally as works of art.

Metal Casts: The Africans also produce fine brass casts with the lost wax process. The tribes known for this art are the Yoruba and Bini in Nigeria, and the Ashanti in Ghana, with their cousins the Baule of the Ivory Coast. Hardly known are the fine casts of the Senufo, the Mossi, and the Kran and Dan. It is rare that you see one of them in a museum.

I could still see the technique, both among the Baule and among the Dan and Kran. The object to be cast is first formed from the wax of wild bees. It is then embedded in clay. This is a complicated process. The clay must be applied in several layers, the first one being the finest. Among the Kran, the clay must be taken from the soil of an old hut. It is mixed with the juice of the leaves of the oil palm, which renders it glutinous, and is then carefully dropped and brushed onto the wax model by means of a feather. Each layer must dry separately. Then the wax is melted out and a second form attached, which contains the metal. The metal is melted over the fire in the smithy, and then the entire clay form is turned around so that the brass flows into the hollow space left by the wax. The form is then broken, yielding in metal the object which had first been formed in wax. The objects are frequently decorated with spirals, concentric circles, or segments of them. These were originally made with a long wax thread which is coiled round and round, then stuck onto the wax model.

The artists who know this craft are usually at the same time blacksmiths, for they need bellows to melt the metal. Most of them are also carvers.

Three Artists of the Dan and Kran

To turn to real human life, I want to introduce three carvers of the Dan and the neighbouring Kran in Liberia. For two of them I shall quote what my son, Eberhard Fischer-Himmelheber, has found out on our last expedition, in 1960.

Zra: The first is old man Zra, the greatest of artists this country has known during the last two generations. There is no greater one in the memory of these people. I knew Zra well, but no longer could he carve. A horrible sickness ravaged his lean tall body. All his wives but one had left him. Zra had been brought to his lonely farm, as the Kran do with the incurably sick. When I arrived, half a dozen people were busy with the newly harvested rice. Zra was lying on a mat in the shade of a hut. At once he rose, saying, "If anyone calls here, it can only be for me. My name *Zra* means *God,*" he began: "thus my people call me, because like God I can create beautiful things with my hands."

Zra had been so famous that the chiefs even of tribes hostile to his people invited him to their residences to carve for them. He would then send a message: "Build me a fine hut in the bush where I can work." When this was done, he would move there with his favorite wife and an apprentice. His wife helped him — which is exceptional; she cut the raw shape of the work to be.

96

"I worked for paramount chief Tjudi in Tuleple. Oh yes, for him I carved about twenty masks, big ladles, game boards and figures. When I had finished with Tjudi I went on to chief Bu, in Tuba. For him I carved a figure with a child on its back. For that he gave me a goat, a sheep, and a large gown. Upon his order I carved a woman to look like his headwife. Then I went on to Deu. A wealthy man there had called me. 'You must carve me a man and a woman, and four large rice dishes for my wives,' said he. Well, I even carved ten of them! And a little stool with four legs. When I had finished, Ba gave me a great big cow and killed a second one, to be eaten in my honor. From what I earned with my carving I bought many women. These I sent to my home town, Beleuale. I gave them to my sons and nephews, who in turn worked my farms with these women. I gave one to my disciple, Quadi."

At the end of our first interview, Zra pulled a bundle out of some corner and carefully unwrapped a beautiful ladle whose handle ended in a carved human hand. "When this sickness came over me, which one of my wives witched on me, I felt that this meant the end of my work. I wanted to carve one last big spoon. On it I carved my sculptor's hand, as it closes itself forever." I treated Zra's sickness with apparent success. As I returned to his farm one day to give him another injection, I found him up and about. When we were seated he brought out the ladle and handed it to me, saying: "Why should I keep it any longer, with its sadly closed hand? You have opened my hand again." I am sorry to add that the improvement did not last. Zra died three months later.

Tame: The two following carvers live in one Dan town. The *plates 33—35* most important of them is Tame, about fifty-five years of age. He is really the leading man of the town, mainly because he is the blacksmith. The blacksmith among the west Africans holds a key position, for he manufactures the tools by which most cultural achievements are reached: the farmer's hoe, the hunter's

Plate 33. The Dan carver Tame, using a knife to carve the details of a head on the handle of a ladle

spear, the circumcision knife, tattoo needles, the carver's adze and knife; which in their turn produce masks and drums and mortars and spoons. Tame is busy with blacksmith's work most of the time, but he is also the leading carver of far and wide:

98

Plate 34. Tame, carver of the Dan tribe of Liberia, smooths the surface of a wooden ladle with a rough leaf

he tattoos, he circumcises, he chisels the teeth of men and women, and he makes the complicated headdresses of the women. Tame also is a very good hunter.

In his youth Tame was a trickster, and he is proud of that.

He related many stories of the little tricks he had played on the good people of his town. Once he needed a little money. So he stopped right in front of a man who was known for his ugly teeth: *"Somebody* has ugly teeth," he said. The man, furious at the insult, complained to the chief. "Why?" said Tame, "I never said *this* man had ugly teeth!" Now it was his turn to feel insulted, for he had been falsely accused. He claimed and received an indemnity.

When my son questioned Tame about his ability in carving, Tame first talked about several magical means which help him in his work as a blacksmith, and others which assist him in carving. One prevents the iron from cracking whilst he works it. Another magic induces people to come and order blacksmith's work, if he is out of orders. In choosing the wood for his carvings Tame also takes magical aspects into account. The wood Gä is good for masks, for this is a tree which has life like an animal or human being. At night time one can see the Gä trees walking about and whispering with one another. Tame added that he has not shown any of his magical means to his sons yet: in this way native craftsmen keep their superiority over the younger generation. The young people think that they cannot really succeed in a profession without the magical knowledge which belongs to it.

Among his ancestors Tame names several carvers. For a while his father taught him; but then he gave him to another carver, Uopie, who must have been an outstanding sculptor. He prefers blacksmith's work to carving. By nature, Tame is a tinkerer. He is happiest if you bring him an old muzzle loader which has long been spoilt, and he will surely fix it again. Although he is an excellent carver, he says, "carving is a craft which I have wasted my time in learning." And so, quite often if someone comes to order a mask from him, he sends him on to Tompieme.

plates 36, 37 *Tompieme:* The third carver is called Tompieme. In appearance, he is a less impressive personality than Tame, more the type of the small man who must make a living by diligence in

100

Plate 35. Dancing with the war wask "Gau," Tame holds an old muzzle loader covered with fetishes

simple work. Tame considers him to be his inferior. This impression is right and it is wrong. Of these two carvers, Tompieme is the one who *loves* to carve. He devotes most of his time to carving. On the other hand, he is not as good a carver as Tame. His works are a little clumsy, and not always works of art. In another art, however, Tompieme is a real artist. He is the finest singer in town, and he composes his music all by himself. "My mother," he relates, "was a very good singer, but she never sang in public. She would sing only when pounding her rice in the evening. People used to stop when passing there, just to listen to her beautiful voice. My father and grandfather were mask dancers, so they, too, were singers. Since these two families are united in me, I was born with good music. That is a gift. Very few are born that way." Tompieme used to come to our house in the evening to have his newest song recorded. Half a dozen fellow singers acted as his choir.

Plate 36. The Dan carver Tompieme begins a mask using an adze

Tompieme's wife, by the way, is a medicine woman of the most respected kind; that is, she owes her qualification to the fact that a spirit revealed itself to her and made her a diviner against her own will. Other medicine men or women often inherit their relation to a spirit, or acquire it by membership in a certain secret society. It speaks for Tompieme that this woman, who was first married to his brother Zame, a most successful hunter and therefore a wealthy man, preferred the poor carver Tompieme to her husband and ran away with him. She suffered hard times for years, until the spirit made itself known to her, and made people come from afar with the finest gifts, in exchange for the spirit's services.

Tompieme relates: "When I was a boy there was only my big brother Uopie with us." [We remember that this was the man who also taught carving to Tame, the great blacksmith.] "If he went to the smithy he asked me to work the bellows for him, and in this way I could watch him at work. Thus I did until he died. After him came Tame and took all his tools, for Uopie had taught him first. One day, while hunting in the bush, I grew tired and slept there. My dead brother Uopie appeared to me in a dream and asked me, 'Why don't you do what I taught you? Why are you just hunting?' The next day I bought an adze in the market. In the following night, my brother again came to me in my dream. 'I bought an adze,' I said to him, 'now what shall I do?' 'Carve a Kagle mask,' the spirit commanded. This I did, and from that day I kept on carving. If a masker's mask had become old and unseemly, I carved him a new one. I took up blacksmith's work, which my brother had also shown me. It had been his habit to work one week as a blacksmith, and spend the next one carving."

Strange remains the relation between Tompieme and Tame, the carver and blacksmith. They had both had the same master, Uopie, and Tame was the first to learn his art from him. At the master's death Tame took all his tools. This fact among others

Plate 37. Tompieme begins to apply the black surface color to a new mask

104

makes him Tompieme's master, and this to an extent which seems grotesque to us. Tompieme can only carve if Tame permits him to do so. If a man arrives from some other town because he wants Tompieme to carve something for him, he must see Tame about it first. Tame will then pass the order on to Tompieme. All the goods that Tompieme earns for his carving he delivers to Tame, who then returns some to him, but sometimes keeps them all for himself. "Some day," says Tompieme, "Tame may call the elders and then publicly speak to me: 'From now onwards you may eat all the goods you are earning by your carving.' Then I shall be free. But why should he do so? That day would be welcome, but I am happy as it is, just the same. Tame gives me respect. I may always use his tools. No master can fight another master. I do not carve to earn something, but mainly for my fame. My name must not be lost when I die. My apprentice Ge will also tell of me when I am dead."

The three artists we have come to know are experts in several occupations. This is characteristic of the African artist. In him, there is nothing of the naiveté so often found and even cultivated with the Western artist. Many Africans think that carving is just a matter of high intelligence.

The artist and convention

Seen in a museum, African art shows considerable variety. If however we travel to Africa and there study the art of *one* certain tribe we observe an astonishing uniformity. Each tribe has its own style. Characteristic of the Bapende style, for example, are slanted lines, fleeing backward from the observer. Chubby faced, round forms are characteristic of the Kran style.

The public wants the artist to keep within the limits of this tribal style, but it may happen that a tribe has two such styles side by side. Thus the Guro on the Ivory Coast have masks which in style are close to that of their eastern neighbours, the Baule; and others in the altogether different style of the northern

Senufo. We do not know why this is so, but it is important to realize that the carvers of this tribe think or feel in two very different tribal styles.

Individuality: As my son found out, we can nevertheless recognize a personal style of each artist. All the Dan artists we came to know have a personal style. In Tame's faces, the nose, among other traits, is characteristic. Zra's works always have a monumental character. His faces are most impressive; there is courage behind his carving; and he has unusual ideas: in one of his masks, which is now in my collection, he tried to carve a face which at the same time should be a hippo's and a man's; not, as African artists usually do, by simply adding a hippo's teeth to a man's face, but by amalgamating the huge face of the hippo with the finer traits of a human being. You will read and see more of these personal styles when my son publishes the results of his investigations among the Dan.

Individuality is most conspicuous in the carving of animals. The human face or figure, so frequently represented in the art of a tribe, has often become conventionalized. For the animals, there is usually no such pattern. Each artist has to find his own way, as we see in three chimpanzee masks of the Kran, carved by three different artists; or on four weaving spools of the Guro, in which four artists tried to represent an elephant's head.

The artist is quite at liberty to show an individual concept in details. It happens that details are fantastically varied until we can no longer recognize what was originally meant. We see this in the headdresses of Senufo figures, which are supposed to represent a certain bird. The public does not, however, ask for individuality as much as we do. The carvers themselves see no wrong in copying one another's work. It happens that a customer says: "Carve me a palm wine cup or a comb, such as carver Kofi made for chief Kouadiobli." For Kofi it is an honour to see his original work so highly appreciated. The artist who is asked to make the copy does not take offense either. One carver in the

106

Cameroons said to me that it was more difficult to copy a piece of carving than to create a new one. From the point of view of skill this may be correct.

Inspiration: When I questioned the artists about the way in which they receive the inspiration for a new object of art, Tompieme said that when looking at the block of wood which he is going to carve he sees the future work in it. The others usually quoted one of two possibilities: to many of them the inspiration comes in a dream, meaning a real night's dream, not a state of trance; or just day dreaming. Some specify that their deceased father or master appears to them in a dream showing them how to carve a certain object.

Some artists have a fetish which furnishes the inspiration. Old Zra told me that he had a fetish for that, and so did the carvers of the Badjokwe in the Congo. In their working place, I saw the Bayaka artists in the Congo planting a little mask which was to inspire them, not by its own form, but in a magical way. Tame said, "if one wants to be famous among the carvers one obtains a certain leaf in the bush. This I pound in a little snuff-mortar, together with dry mud which I scratch from a house wall. From this mixture I form little sausages with pointed ends. With these I rub my hands before I begin to carve. Then this magic shows me all the different forms of masks and spoons which men have ever made. They show up in my head *like something coming to the surface of the water.*"

Portraits: If we look at these rigid, extremely stylized faces we can hardly imagine that they could be meant to portray certain individuals. Yet this is often the case. An ancestor figure is supposed to represent a certain dead person. A mask, too, is often carved to the likeness of some certain person just to make sure that it will look nice. The African readily recognizes such a portrait. The likeness lies, not, as has been written, in certain attributes like hairdress or tattooing. It is really the *traits* of the face which are carved in wood and convey the likeness. Old man

107

Zra, the great carver who was called by the chiefs to carve for them, once got in trouble carving a portrait. "Whilst carving for this chief," he relates, "I fell in love with one of his younger women. I carved her face on a big ladle and took it home to remember her. When my headwife saw that spoon she asked sharply: 'What's that?' 'Oh,' I replied quickly, 'I carved that for you, and handed her the spoon."

Magical reasons may prevent a carver from carving the likeness of a certain person. One Guro carver said: "I am afraid to carve the face of a particular man or girl, for if that person should die soon after, people might attribute the death to this portrait."

We are surprised to see that the faces of African sculptures often do not show the characteristics of the African face: the nose is slender, the lips thin, the face oval. If I asked the Africans what their ideal of a beautiful face was, it turned out they prefer traits which are rather the contrary of the typical African face: a good-looking man or woman must have small, slim, delicately cut features. Now we know that for at least fifteen hundred years belligerent tribes from the Near East have moved into Africa, conquered the Negro peasants in many regions, and remained as their rulers. To this day we often find pointedly non-African types in the chiefs' families. It is likely that the Africans have formed their ideal of beauty after this foreign aristocracy. This would explain the non-African appearance of so many African sculptures.

The faces of African carvings usually show no expression. We must be very careful not to lend them our own interpretation, as is often done by photographic effects in our books on Negro art. A mask often seems to us most expressive; yet when I asked the artist in such a case what expression he had intended to give to his work he usually hesitated and had to think for a while, for he had not intended any expression at all. Then he might name an expression quite different from what appeared to me.

A mask which appears to us to be opening its mouth in suffering or wailing, may appear to an African to be laughing, because it shows its teeth as we do in smiling.

Now, when we see a masked person performing, we realize that one certain expression on the face of the mask would in most cases be quite out of place. The mask whilst in action takes different roles, each of which would afford a different expression. The Ngedi mask of the Dan, which imitates all sorts of people of its village in different actions, and also rice birds and mischievous monkeys, changes its supposed expression every minute. It is quite a strange experience when we see the mask performing, as we seem to observe all the different expressions which belong to its various actions. The mask shows curiosity, takes pity on someone, threatens the spectators. This being so, the artist gives the mask a neutral expression and leaves the interpretation to the imagination of the spectator.

Art for aesthetic purposes only: What is, among the Africans, the importance of the sculptures as works of art? With masks and figures, the aesthetic quality is only of secondary importance. These objects are made for a certain spiritual purpose. If the carvers were not artists, they would be made without art, crudely; but they would still be made. As a matter of fact I have seen two tribes in Gabun whose masks cannot rate as works of art; yet they served their purpose.

It is different in applied art, where art is an *attribute* having nothing to do with the use of the object. Art in these objects may even be quite a nuisance when the object is put to use. I own an African flybrush whose handle ends in the figure of a bird which grabs a snake winding itself round the handle to attack the bird. When chasing the flies with this flybrush the owner must be very careful not to break the delicate carving. The same is the case with the famous weaving spool of the Baule and Guro. This implement holds a pulley between its two shanks. It hangs on the weaver's loom, just in front of his eyes, and is therefore adorned with some fine little head. Very often one of the shanks breaks off under the strain which is exerted on the pulley, so that it has to be nailed on again. I once asked a weaver why he did not make this tool cheaper and more durable out of some iron hook. "Well," he replied, "one does not want to live without the pretty things."

So here, even in applied art, art is employed only for its own sake. It is not quite free, however, inasmuch as it is still bound to a certain useful object — a spoon, a flybrush — which is meant to decorate, and which to some extent prescribes its form.

There exists in Africa also the independent object of art which is created for its own sake only. I have found this among five tribes: the Dan, the Kran, the Baule, the Bakuba, and in the Cameroon Grassland. These objects are not permanently exhibited in the owner's house, but are kept in a bag or basket to be shown only occasionally, as the Japanese do with their paintings.

Among the Dan, where they are of brass, they are placed near the fire where a newcomer will see them at once. We see animals such as a crocodile, frog, or lizard, carved in wood or cast in metal. Among the Baule we discover strange things: a wooden bugle, carved exactly like the wooden bugle which they use for signalling: same size, same ornaments, but it is *massive*, so that you cannot blow it! As if to emphasize this uselessness, an ornament is carved in the place where the opening should be. Or from another tribe, the Bakuba in the Congo, two boxes for red body paint. We can lift the cover of one of them to put the paint inside, but the other one is solid — the lid does not come off. What does this mean? It means that some of these African tribesmen think the objects which they carve for their daily use are so beautiful that they deserve to be raised to the sphere of pure art. The bugle, the powderbox left solid, cannot be enslaved to a practical purpose.

110